30p

Promises of Hope

Barbara Honour

Foreword by

Rev. George B. Duncan

Christian Focus Publications Ltd.

Published by
Christian Focus Publications Ltd.
Geanies House
Fearn, Tain
Ross-shire IV20 1TW
Scotland

ISBN 0 906731 72 0

Printed and bound in Great Britain by
Cox & Wyman Ltd., Reading

Foreword

No book in the Bible records so vividly the needs of the human heart as it tries to cope with the varying pressures and circumstances of life as the Book of Psalms. Wherever we start to read, sooner or later we find a word that speaks to our situation at that moment! In this book Barbara Honour has selected certain verses that have obviously meant much to her, and with spiritual insight and practical application to the realities of life, has brought to each day a message that will give encouragement to the reader. The Bible claims that it will be a lamp to our feet and shed light upon our path! I am confident that the sincere seeker will find that to be true, and trust that then the reader will find grace sufficient to meet the need of the moment.

By George B. Duncan

———————

All author's royalties will go to International Christian radio programmes.

DAY 1

Psalm 1, v.3

He shall be like a tree planted by the rivers of water . . . .

Here we are at the beginning of this marvellous book of Psalms, and this first message to us has been titled, 'The Pursuit of Happiness'. Happiness! Surely this is what we are all seeking in this life? How strange that the verses begin with three negatives! We read that the one who is blessed of God does not walk in the counsel of unbelievers, does not stand in the way of sinners and does not sit in the company of scoffers. See how progressive the thoughts are — walks, stands, and finally, sits. But we see the man or woman in pursuit of true happiness as a positive person. These are the folk who daily search the Word of God; they find absolute delight as they give time and meditation to each precious Word. We hear much of 'meditation' as a cult symbol in these days, but one wonders at the value of such exercise apart from the study of God's eternal Word freely given, in our Bibles.

The positive believer takes hold of God's promises and finds his life becomes fertile, 'like a tree planted by the rivers of water'. What a picture! A green tree, bearing fruit, whose roots are deep down into God's rich soil. No dry, withered leaves or dead fruit on this tree; it flourishes, gives beauty to the eye and shade for others to enjoy.

This is a picture of a fulfilled, happy life, bearing the manifold fruit of the Holy Spirit. We see a

Christian character that is radiant, attractive, bringing glory to God.

How about the promise that we may enter into, contained in verse 3? If we will take heed to the warnings in the negatives we considered in verse 1, and make the Word of God our daily diet, then we shall rejoice in this promise:—

'Whatsoever he does shall prosper'.

Marvellous! Believe it.

Try this way and you will find it a good recipe for life.

Jesus said, 'He that believes on me, out of his inmost being shall flow rivers of Living Water' *(John 7, v.38).*

Be a river Christian!

DAY 2

Psalm 89, v.1

I will sing of the mercies of the Lord for ever . . . .

Let us begin our day with a song. The Psalmist tells us he will sing of the mercies of the Lord for ever. So if you and I are among that great company of people who love God and have tasted of His goodness, we too will sing of His mercies in Eternity.

So we should begin now and get in practice, for there's a real need in this poor world for a good song, a faithful testimony to our wonderful God, to be heard.

'For who in Heaven can be compared to the Lord? Who among the sons of the mighty can be likened to the Lord?' What a question! We read in this psalm about opening our mouth and speaking to all generations . . . . while we may. Surely the young ones need to hear about the reality, the guidance, the power of the Living Lord Jesus.

And who can tell them but those who have tasted of His mercy and forgiveness through many changing scenes? When we consider senior citizens among us, we know there is some social care provided, but think of the famine of the word of God all around them, the need of assurance and heart comfort that these 'special' dear ones need at eventide. So let them hear your song of experience and testimony. 'I'm not a singer', you may say. No?

but you and I are excellent 'talkers'. Speak a word for Jesus to-day, will you? Make known His faithfulness to *all* generations.

'Let the redeemed of the Lord say so, whom he has redeemed from the hand of the enemy' *(Psalm 107, v.2).*

DAY 3

Psalm 27, v.14

Wait on the Lord: be of good courage, and he shall strengthen thine heart: wait, I say, on the Lord.

I'm not very good at waiting — I live like you do, in days of 'Instant' this and that, 'Instant Tea and Coffee' and instant contact as I ring telephone numbers.

Yes, it's a wonderful world, yet it's all going a bit too fast for most of us, and so we feel extreme pressures, and anxieties. In this lovely psalm we have David, who knew much of fears, wars, and deadly terrors, exhorting us to wait on the Lord. This is the same God who delivered King David from frightful oppression and 'brought him into a large place', as he tells us in another psalm.

Then he says to us, (and this is for every day and

age) 'Be of good courage and God will strengthen your heart'. This is not an instant package of courage handed to us, rather it's a challenge to you and me to summon up the courage within, to have no fear as we recall the words of Jesus Himself. 'Be not afraid', He said so many times, because He is on the Throne and God alone is able to make our heart strong.

Note the word 'wait' which David feels the need to repeat, as he says 'wait, I say on the Lord'. What does this mean? I would say it means we are not to run before the Lord reveals His peaceful plan for our lives. In quietness and confidence shall be your strength. As we wait upon God, the heartbeats slow down to a quiet rest and tempo. In this quietness, our God will surely speak and we shall know it is Him. One of old declared, 'I, being in the way, the Lord led me'. *(Genesis 24, v.27)*.

DAY 4

Psalm 35, v.20

Them that are quiet in the land.

Are there still some quiet folk in the land? Has our world developed only into harsh, intrusive shouts and voices? Must we be overwhelmed with vibrant discord each time we turn a certain knob? Praise God we can turn that knob the other way: we make our choice. And, yes! there are those that are quiet in the land. The hidden ones who praise and pray, who meet God in the early morning and are refreshed. They have a word to share with weary, storm-tossed ones they will surely meet.

I discover such quiet ones as I look into my Bible. I see the girl who was to be the great-grandmother to King David and I find Ruth as a lowly gleaner in the barley field. Quiet as a harvest mouse! Her name is right there in Matthew 1, in the immortal genealogy of great David's greater Son! I see a little maid in the grand household of Naaman, Syrian general but a leper. And what is she doing? She is speaking of her God, and of His prophet Elisha, who could bring healing. So this blessing came to Naaman, through 'a quiet one' and she, nameless, is in our Holy Bible!

I can feel too, the quietness among the shepherds keeping their sheep around Bethlehem, when the Glory of God broke into the silent night and they heard the choir of angels! A Saviour was born!

It is at such times when you and I are among the quiet ones in the land that we do, indeed, touch the Glory and the world recedes. We find it is true, for

God Himself has said this, 'Be still and know that I am God'. No matter what tumults and clamourings are all about us, we have an unchanging God- . . . . who is always there.

'There is a place of quiet rest near to the heart of God'.

DAY 5

Psalm 42, v.3

They continually say unto me, Where is thy God?

David, in this psalm, is speaking to his own soul; he is asking, 'Why are you cast down? Why so depressed?' And he tells of his tears continually, day and night. In the opening verses we see he is longing and thirsting for God . . . . 'as a thirsty hart pants for the water', is the picture he paints. This David who knew such joy as he praised God; as he worshipped and sang with a great congregation on holy days, now has a very 'down' day and in this state of depression he is taunted by unbelievers around him. They speedily resort to their favourite cry; 'Where is your God?'

I wonder if you find more help in David's depressions than in his constant praise? If you do, you are looking at a real natural man in these psalms, reminding us of our Lord Jesus who, we are told, 'was tempted in all points as we are, yet without sin'. So we see David in his moods of torment and thirsting after God, just like you and me. Only Christ was more sorely tempted and sinned not.

In the closing verses of Psalm 42 there are four little words — 'Hope thou in God', and David confidently says, 'I shall yet praise Him, who will give a shine to my face. He is my God'. And this can happen before the dark day is through. Recognise depression as the oppression of the enemy of your soul. 'Resist him and he will fly from you', writes James in chapter 4, v.8. Peter also knew his onslaughts. He exhorts Christians to 'Resist him, steadfast in the faith' *(1 Peter 5, v.8,9)*.

Before the day is through, you will be praising. You are not alone in your experience; these battle scenes we must all pass through; 'but God is faithful, who will not suffer you to be tempted above that you are able; but will with the temptation also make a way to escape' *(1 Cor. 10, v.13)*.

DAY 6

Psalm 23, v.1

The Lord is my Shepherd; I shall not want.

We must talk together of this favourite Psalm. We sing it in our churches, some of us learnt it in our school days, most folk are so familiar with these words, ' The Lord is my Shepherd'. 'Oh yes,' people say, 'It's my favourite psalm.' In some cases, it's the only one they have ever known!

And yet, it's a great statement to say, 'I am in His flock, the Lord leads me, and I know I shall never want, because I'm trusting Him. He has restored my soul and led me into a perfect peace.' This speaks of one who has known the safety, certainty, and security of God's salvation all the days of his life, and there are so many millions all over the world who can say that this is real and true.

Perhaps the greatest verse is the last one which speaks of assurance that the believer will dwell in the house of the Lord for ever! This is tremendous, to be sure of this and the truth is that such security is possible. Possible — and available for the one who comes to God's dear Son, the Lord Jesus Christ, and takes Him as personal Saviour and Shepherd through life.

How you and I need to be sure of definite guidance in every phase of our lives, don't we? Then we shall fear no evil, although we now live in an increasingly evil world, for there is Divine guidance and protection in the Living Person of Jesus. *(John 16, v.13; Psalm 32, v.8).*

On so many occasions this psalm is chosen to be sung because perhaps the tune is familiar or folk

13

have no idea what to choose, especially on the last solemn occasion. And yet, to sing 'The Lord is my Shepherd' when we have never submitted to His Way and His Truth in our life, is to sing a dreadful un-truth. We praise God for His mercy for there is time — even today — to put the matter right, to make the risen Jesus our true Shepherd who leads into everlasting Life. Read John's Gospel chapter 10. There's no other way.

Christ himself is the Way, the Truth, and the Life. *(John 14, v.6)*.

DAY 7

Psalm 138, v.1

I will praise thee with my whole heart.

I like this; it speaks of being whole-hearted. There is much apathy in our church gatherings, much that is just half-hearted. The fact is, in modern days, there is everything to distract our minds, to use up our energy, and to wear us out with worry concerning material things, so that many men and women are not seeking to find the Living God with their whole heart at all!

They may say, like Job of old, 'O that I knew where I may find Him!' Or it may be, 'How can you know that Jesus is alive to-day?'. The answer is all in the Book. Way back, in the days of Jeremiah, God gave the clue to this question. In Jeremiah 29, v.13 we read, 'And you shall seek Me and find Me when you shall search for Me with all your heart.' That's it! Be whole-hearted and you shall find God. Better still, you may even know Him, and you will find that God was in Christ, reconciling the world to Himself. 'He that has seen Me,' said Jesus 'has seen the Father', *John 14;* read all this enlightening chapter.

Did I say that we may know Him? Paul said this: 'That I may know Him and the Power of His Resurrection' *(Philippians 3, v.10)*, and this he wrote as an older man, still wholehearted in his seeking to know God. 'And this is life eternal that they might know thee the only true God, and Jesus Christ whom thou hast sent', writes John in chapter 17, v.3 of his gospel.

There is one true God, and you and I may seek Him and find Him, in the face of the altogether lovely One, the Lord Jesus Christ.

Men seek for gold, treasures, glory, adventure, with all their might and main. Seek for the great and lasting treasure, even Jesus, with your whole heart.

DAY 8

Psalm 126, v.2

Then was our mouth filled with laughter, and our tongue with singing.

There are men and women who are afraid to open the Bible. They expect to read only of doom and gloom. Convicted of their neglect of the Way of Salvation, they shun the Book entirely. What a sad, sad loss in life — to miss the joy and comfort the Word of God gives to a believer; how amazed many would be to discover laughter within its pages! Here it is in this psalm, written about a people who had been rescued by God out of captivity. 'We were like them that dream!' they are telling us. 'We were filled with laughter and we sang for joy!' Those who heard them could only say one thing — 'The Lord has done great things for them'. He surely had! Released from oppression and captivity, they remembered their tears — now turned to joy.

What a picture of those of us who, once convicted of our neglect of God and our independence of Him, heard of full and free forgiveness because Christ had died in our place. As soon as we believed this and received Him as our Saviour from sin, we began to feel the freedom of a New Life in Christ. Then we felt light as air; as Christians we could laugh and sing together freely. 'Truly, they have something to sing about!' might be the comment of our neighbours.

In the ancient book of Nehemiah we read that he, too, had found the answer. 'The joy of the Lord is your strength' *(Nehemiah 8, v.10)*. Are you feeling weak in body today believer?, the joy of the Lord is for you especially.

An expression these days is 'to fall about, laughing'. How surprising to read in Genesis 17, v.17 that Abraham did just this! 'Then Abraham fell upon his face and *laughed*.' Nothing new under the sun, is there? So his son was called Isaac, which means 'laughter', for he was born when his father was 100 years old! Our God is the God of Abraham, *Isaac*, and Jacob. He is the God who gives His children —

Laughter and Joy!

DAY 9

Psalm 107, v.6

Then they cried unto the Lord in their trouble, and He delivered them out of their distresses.

There are two choruses that are repeated several times in this psalm-to-be-sung. One is the cry of the Lord and the answering one is the chorus of praise, for the two go together: the cry of the human heart and the praise that should follow. I say 'should' follow for we meet many folk who will plead for prayer-help in their distress, but we do not have them coming back to *praise* when our gracious King answers! As Christians we need to be careful to give God the glory.

So we have this delightful chorus:— 'Let the redeemed of the Lord say so, whom He has redeemed from the hand of the enemy.' One can recall another saying of David's — 'He has plucked my feet out of the net'. A vivid picture here, of entangled feet set free! Free to walk with God.

In this psalm we are right up to date, as we look at wanderers in the wilderness of this world. It has always been a dry, tempting, wilderness filled with plastic imitations that have never, never satisfied the heart-hunger of men and women. So they wander through, trying everything, hungry and thirsty in their soul, near fainting. Then comes the cry to God . . . . not to a man or to an idol!

Verses 6, 13, 19, 28 all repeat the powerful refrain:— 'He saved them out of their distresses.' 'He sent His word and healed them and delivered them from their destructions . . . . He blessed them also, so that they are multiplied greatly.'

You must read the whole psalm; it will lift up your heart; you will find yourself joining in the chorus, 'O that men would praise the Lord for His goodness, and for His wonderful works to the children of men!' For in Christ He saves and satisfies. Is that your testimony? We need many more to join this band of joyful pilgrims who are not afraid to

'Say so!'

DAY 10

Psalm 45, v.1

Touching the King.

My heart is bubbling up with a good matter, writes the psalmist, as he leads us into the palace of the King in this psalm. Men, women and teenagers in these perilous times are looking for a powerful leader. Here one can see King Jesus, mighty, victorious, triumphant over His enemies. He wields the sword and the sceptre; token of His Majesty and judgment! And He is gracious and blessed of God for ever and ever. No passing potentate is this Eternal One. We see Him again in Revelation 19. John 'saw Heaven opened and, behold a white horse and He that sat upon it was called Faithful and True, and in righteousness He judges and makes war.' This is the final great war with the enemies of God, and the Lord Christ wears a vesture dipped in blood. The cost of His victory is in the shed blood of His Cross. There He bore our sins in His own body on the tree. There, the victory over Satan and sin was proclaimed openly, for all to see.

You will note the mention of myrrh and aloes in this prophetic psalm, symbols of the bitterness of His sacrificial death. But there is the fragrance of His very garments mentioned, too, in verse 8.

Then there are the King's daughters. We are told they are 'all-glorious within'. How can this be? I am not so, you are not so, for we are all born in sin and we cannot make ourselves clean. We could never be princesses, daughters of this mighty King! But the warm love of God the Father reached down to you and me, in the Person of Jesus. Has this reached your needy heart, so that you know you really are — by faith all-glorious within?

John 1, v.12 says: 'But as many as received Him, to them gave He power to become the sons of God, even to them that believe on His name.'

DAY 11

Psalm 51, v.7

Wash me, and I shall be whiter than snow.

God desires truth in the inward parts and our Christian faith is an inward faith, founded upon the tremendous blessing of a clean heart. Only our God can do this. As we look into Luke's gospel we see the Lord Jesus sadly watching a rich young ruler turning away from revealed truth. Peter, standing by, asks the great question, 'Who then can be saved?' Who, indeed? But the One who is Himself the Way and the Truth gives the answer, 'The things which are impossible with men are possible with God'. Our God is able!

David, who wrote Psalm 51, knew this great mystery, revealed to him by the Holy Spirit way back in time. It's all there in this psalm, as we see David coming to God, deep in his sin, and he cries, 'Have mercy upon me, O God'. Then, as he acknowledges his transgressions, his consciousness of being unclean before a Holy God, he proceeds to ask God to do everything for him, deep down. I want you to note the active verbs. 'Wash me', 'Purge me', 'Make me', 'Hide Thy face from my sins', 'Create in me a clean heart', 'Renew a right spirit', 'Restore to me the joy of Thy salvation', 'Deliver me'.

Oh that we might cease from our striving to be better men and women! That we might see our need,
(1) of the mercy of God and then, (2) to begin to ask our mighty God, who is filled with loving kindness and tender mercies, to do for us that deep work that

is needed in our hearts, by His Holy Spirit.

Is it true that we have lost our first love? Grown careless, loveless, because the way has been hard? Has God revealed to us how we have some lack and lost our cutting edge of witness? Are we like David, deep in sin and need to call this by it's name? This psalm is here, so precious, so essential for every Christian and anyone seeking salvation. God Himself will do for you and me what we can never do for ourselves.

In Psalm 50 God speaks to David in these words: 'Call upon me in the day of trouble; I will deliver you and then you shall glorify me.'

DAY 12

Psalm 46, v.5

God is in the midst of her; she shall not be moved.

This is a strong psalm of comfort and assurance. It is for everyone, but for some of us it is the 'Ladies' psalm'. Here we have a word to tell us that 'God is in the midst of her; she shall not be moved'. We have the time (in the KJV margin) given and this is 'when the morning appears'. As I write this message, the freshness of a perfect June morning is blessing my own heart, and I look at a list of names of many women friends for whom I have prayed. All these have passed through a time of deep distress, some sickness, many in depression or bitterness of soul. For these the promise has been claimed . . . . 'God shall help her and that right early'. . . . And there is my pencil tick beside many dear names. For others, one awaits fulfilment. My Saviour, who alone is Mighty and able to deliver, He sees that He is trusted and we look for fulfilment of this precious Word.

'I will not let you go unless You bless me' said that old Jacob man. What a rascal he was, but how God loved him because he held on grimly, in his tremendous time of trouble, to the power of his God! Yes, he obtained mercy and won through to victory. This one so like us in his devious character, yet became Israel, a prince with God. How amazing, that the Lord loved him and did not despise him for holding on till the blessing came!

So we have this word for today. 'The Lord of hosts is with us: the God of Jacob is our refuge'. Yes indeed, a word tried and proved. Through many tough patches a present help in trouble. Therefore we will not fear: though the earth be removed, and the mountains shake. 'Selah' is written here. Take note! Sooner or later you and I will need this strong word again.

DAY 13

Psalm 116, v.1

I love the Lord because He hath heard my voice and my supplications.

Because He has inclined His ear unto me God has heard my voice calling upon Him! Of all the voices in all the great wide world, people of all colours and races crying out to Almighty God . . . . yet He has heard MY voice! No wonder the psalmist says 'Therefore will I call upon Him as long as I live'.

The writer here is not one of the negative folk who tell us 'It's no use praying!' This one who loves God has been down even to the sorrows of death and the pains of hell, and has found trouble and sorrow. So we may conclude that he knows what God can do: there is experience here. 'I was brought low and He helped me', he writes. Can you say this? Can I? Indeed, I can, and I remember well the many times my heart has rejoiced when my cry has been heard and wonderfully answered, and, sometimes, it has been only a cry — even a sigh! And it has been heard in Heaven. To call on the Name of Jesus when one is in a tight spot and there is no time for words brings all the power of Heaven to one's aid. There is no greater Name.

Three vital points are shown in verse 8 of this sweet psalm: the soul delivered from death, the eyes from tears, and the feet from falling. What is your present need? Can it be you need assurance that your precious soul is saved and that you are 'right with God' as we say? Heart-belief and complete trust in Christ's finished work on the Cross will bring this to you. You may sing with the great congregation then, 'It is well, it is well with my soul'. Our God is able to do this for you. Then tears will be dried, for God Himself will wipe away all tears from our eyes, and soon, when Jesus reigns — forever! Now, to walk the Christian way, He will even keep our feet from falling!

Oh, join with me in this psalm of praise and tell the world why you love the Lord. He wants you to take the cup of salvation and keep calling upon His Name!

DAY 14

Psalm 3, v.3

The Lifter up of my head

You might think that David was writing in our present-day idiom when he described his God as 'The lifter up of my head'. I am reminded of an early radio programme which began the day with a series called 'Lift up your hearts'. The Word of God was broadcast and listeners knew their hearts were lifted up.

So we have in this psalm the picture of the Lord Himself as a shield, a protector against the enemy, and this we recognise as being a part of the Christian's armour. The Shield of Faith! Take this, we read in Ephesians chapter 6 verse 16, take this piece of armour above all, to quench those fiery darts of the enemy. The shield can be moved from place to place, wherever the attack may come. When the battle is raging, remember the Sword of the Spirit, which is the Word of God.

If you are reading your Bible constantly, day in and day out, you are surely discovering that this Living Word has become part of your subconscious self; it has been woven into your memory by the Holy Spirit and He is the One who will bring the Word to mind in time of need. This is a fact, promised by our Lord Jesus, *(John 14, v.26)* This is how we can discover — with David — that God Himself is our Shield, our Glory, and the lifter-up of our head.

When your heart is heavy and your feet seem to drag because you are oppressed and even daily chores seem irksome; then is the time to seek and read again this testimony of one who suffered the torment of deadly enemies and knew even rebellion and treachery in his own son Absalom. Yes, King David knew what he was writing about when he tells us 'God is my shield, my glory, and the lifter-up of my head'.

DAY 15

Psalm 119, v.11

Thy Word have I hid in mine heart,

Now here is a psalm to study! We could take many books and fill them all with precious thoughts expressed in this longest psalm. The writer is one who loves God's Word, to him it is very pure, tried or refined like gold in a furnace. This living Word has quickened new life in the psalmist, so he has wisely hidden it in a safe place — in his heart, that he might be kept from sinning against God's laws. I have a sweet memory of a man's clear tenor voice as he sang in a well-known choir and the words still ring with power. He sang, 'It's in my heart, this melody of love divine, it's in my heart, since I am His and He is mine!' Sincerity there, and the song in the power of the Holy Spirit lingers still in my memory.

The psalmist writes in verse 31 about his 'stickability', He says: 'I have stuck unto Thy testimonies O Lord put me not to shame!' Like a stamp stuck on a letter and given a thump with the fist, so this man shows decision, committal and determination to live for God. That's what we want to see in our younger Christians today: we long to see their whole-hearted determination to stand for Jesus Christ. It's so easy to come forward, moved by the Spirit in a powerful crusade. This is exciting and encouraging for those who are older, but with the great need for young converts to 'stay the course' and to develop this 'stickability' there's a clear call for wise teaching and, above all, for faithful, upholding prayer. Surely somebody prayed earnestly for you and for me, or we'd never be so close to our Saviour today! We could still be in the creche, in an immature baby stage of our Christian life, without that faithful prayer.

Let me exhort you to continue in prayer for our young ones — the V.I.P's of our day. They are in need of this upholding.

DAY 16

Psalm 119, v.63

I am a companion of all them that fear Thee.

In the book of Malachi there is a verse that seems to be quiet and secret, not often quoted. It's in chapter 3, v.16 'Then they that feared the Lord spoke often to one another; the Lord listened and heard it, and a book of remembrance was written before Him for them that feared the Lord and that thought upon His Name'.

Well! who are your close friends? Are you a companion of all those whom you know love the Lord? I believe the happiest times for all Christians are when we are together and able to freely share what the Lord has been doing in our lives, how He has answered the smallest and the greatest prayer, how He has specially blessed us! Most of us have also experienced some empty days and hours in the company of others who do not know the Lord Jesus; to whom we could not speak of His Name, because we are well aware that they are among that great multitude of people to-day who do not want to know. Jesus did speak clearly to His disciples about pearls and where we should not cast them, so we know well when to be silent. This is a sad situation and it happens to most of us even within our own family, does it not? It indicates a need for us to get praying, so that the ground of their hearts may be broken up, made ready for the sowing of His precious seed. Truly, each one of us has need of patience, and God will give it. The Lord will provide the burden of care and prayer, the breaking up of the soil, and His own word to be

33

sown at the right moment in time. We must believe this, then a harvest will surely come.

So let us enjoy the strength of Christian fellowship when we may. Notice, in God's library there is this Book of Remembrance, in which there are recorded certain names. Whose are these? They that feared the Lord and thought upon His Name. How wonderful that our God should be so gracious!

DAY 17

Psalm 7, v.9

Oh let the wickedness of the wicked come to an end!

How many times has this thought come into the minds of Christian men and women. How up to date are these feelings expressed by David in his psalms. As we read these words, the longing for the wickedness in this present world system to come to an end is very deep; our emotions are exhausted every day as we hear and see the horrific happenings on the news media.

'God is angry with the wicked every day!,' David writes in verse 11. A powerful sermon was once preached in our local church on this theme; some in the congregation were displeased. Discussing the message afterwards with a young woman who was living life according to her own ideas, I discovered the modern thought concerning love. To love others, to care and to share with all colours, races and life-styles was the worthy theme expressed.

But this same young person, when presented with the great first command given by Christ Himself — to love the Lord God with all the heart, mind, and strength — was indignant and fiercely offended. That God should be angry with the creatures He had made and to whom He had revealed Himself in Jesus Christ produced this strong reaction. This we know, is the offence of the Cross. The apostle Paul wrote about it in *1 Corinthians 1, v.23*. 'Unto the Jews a stumbling block and unto the Greeks foolishness'.

We praise God if to-day we know Christ crucified to be the power of God and 'made to us wisdom, righteousness and sanctification and redemption' *(1 Corinthians 1, v.30)*. The greatest thing in this whole wide world is to know the love of Christ which passes knowledge. Our greatest discovery is to know how to extend that love, because, it is His love coming through our human hearts. It is Calvary love that seeks to love and adore the God who made us, the Father who came Himself — in the Person of Christ, to reconcile us poor sinners to Himself.

Yes, this Holy God is angry with the wicked every day. Why? Because these human creatures seek to by-pass their Great Creator and choose to worship the work of their own hands. Filthy idols — yes! They come in a multitude of forms.

'Little children, keep yourselves from idols' warns the Apostle John.

(1 John, 5, v.21).

DAY 18

Psalm 13, v.1

How long wilt thou forget me, O Lord?

'From sighing to singing' would be a good title for this short psalm. In just six verses we can share in a soul struggle that David experienced from deep agitation in verse 1, when he cries out, 'How long will you forget me O Lord? Forever?' to the last verse when we find he is singing! Why? Because of the way God has dealt with him in his distress. 'He has dealt bountifully with me' says David.

We can picture other heroes of the faith, like Daniel, with good reason to suspect that God had forgotten him, that the end had come when he stood in that den of lions! We know that he was rescued, unscratched by even a lion's claw! Daniel had three friends who had declared, before a pagan King that 'Our God is able to deliver us!' And He did, even from the fiery furnace. Not a hair of their heads was singed, no smell of burning was upon them.

There was a secret Presence with these men who trusted God. The King Nebuchadnezzar declared that he saw the form of a fourth man in that fire. 'The form of the fourth is like the Son of God' was his testimony.

Christ was there in that den of lions with Daniel and with his three friends in that furnace of fire. He was there when David cried out in his affliction. He has said to all believers 'I will never leave you nor forsake you'. *(Hebrews 13, v.5)*. If you are in any fire of affliction today, in any form whatsoever . . . . you too, my friend, may be set free, be assured that God has NOT forgotten. Our times are in His hands, He has the whole *world* in His hands. He will turn your sigh into a song of praise!

DAY 19

Psalm 103, v.4

For He knoweth our frame, He remembereth that we are dust.

There is someone who is very dear to me, and as he grows older and wiser, I often find him saying, 'I am not surprised', in answer to some outstanding bit of news! As we think of it, I trust we do live and learn, watching the behaviour of people and leaders — even governments in this world. We are not surprised at the outcome of events, near and far. There's another wonderful truth I have discovered God the Almighty, the All-knowing One is not surprised at anything I do, or the weak and foolish way I behave . . . . quite often! Not surprised? Why? David knew the answer and he tells us in this wonderful psalm that his God, and our God, is as a beloved Father, He pities His children, those of us poor weak humans who fear Him.

We are not mere things that have happened (or evolved) in this world, as some would have us believe. God made us with His own hands. 'I have created him for my glory, I have formed him, yes I have made him.' Isaiah the prophet wrote this in chapter 43, v.7 and again we have the definite Word of God in chapter 44, which repeats this basic truth, 'Thus saith the Lord that made you and formed you from the womb, who will help you!' This verse continues to speak to Jacob, weak forefather of the erring nation of Israel. Here, we have the words, 'Fear not, my servant whom I have chosen'.

Of course, our Heavenly Father knows the weakness of our poor flesh, He remembers that we are dust, writes David. If you and I are disappointed in ourselves is it not because we have forgotten how weak and sinful we really are? 'Without me', Jesus said, 'you can do nothing'. Nothing!! Nothing that is worthwhile in the sight of a Holy God. Nothing that will stand in the light of Eternity. Without faith, we are told in Hebrews 11, it is impossible to please God. No wonder we fail time and time and time again, until we get sick and tired of our ways.

When you reach such a real low, rock-bottom view of yourself, just take a look at this psalm and begin to bless the Lord for all His Mercy. He forgives, He heals, He redeems our precious soul. He will crown you with loving kindness and tender mercies. All this and more when He gave us His dear Son Jesus Christ to be our Saviour.

DAY 20

Psalm 86, v.5

For thou Lord, art good and ready to forgive; and plenteous in mercy unto all them that call upon Thee.

Yesterday I heard the question in a radio broadcast — 'How many Christian people in our churches really know their God?' This set me thinking. What answers would a questionnaire on the Holy character of God reveal? Beyond the obvious 'God is love' syndrome, I fear there would be few churchgoers who could compile as many as 21 points concerning His royal loveliness. But David does, in this psalm 86, plus 9 points about himself and a further 9 observations concerning nations of his world. This is a good exercise to challenge my reader with today, better far than a crossword puzzle! So your mind will be filled with good positive thinking.

In the first verse we discover that our God has ears! 'Bow down thine ear, O Lord', prays David. Then a word about himself, 'For I am poor and needy'. He is coming with his problems and depression and he is crying to a merciful God — daily. He is making his troubles known in Heaven, he is off-loading his distress to a God who is full of compassion, patient and ready to forgive, full of mercy and truth. No need to cover up our sinfulness and shortcomings when we know such a Saviour, is there? We can give a name to every sin in His presence and thus find relief. Like the pilgrim whom Bunyan pictured with a great load on his back, we too, may come to that Cross of Christ and leave our burden there. Be sure, be very sure to do this; take care not to lift it up again; faith leaves the burden with this merciful, understanding Saviour.

'Show me a token for good' is the final request our psalmist makes in the last verse. This we can pray for ourselves, and more importantly — for others. The God we are getting to know, is One who has ears and who delights to help and comfort! Our critics will become ashamed as they see a Christian life giving all the Glory to God, as David is careful to do.

DAY 21

Psalm 139, v.6

Such knowledge is too wonderful for me.

A medical missionary writing from the starvation situation in Africa today, tells of the cold fear that sometimes grips the heart. Yes, in the intense heat of that climate, there can be cold fear and need of assurance to the child of God, and need of the certainty of His Presence. And this is the psalm to which this young man turns. He is assured that there is no place on earth 'where God is not'. Indeed our psalmist tells us that if he takes 'the wings of the morning and ascends to heaven or makes his bed in hell . . . . God is there'. He is there in the deepest parts of the sea. If he trusts that darkness will hide him from the eyes of God, even the night will be as light about him! No wonder he gasps as he writes 'Such knowledge is too wonderful for me'. Yes, and for me too. 'It is high, I cannot attain it'.

In this wonderful world in which we live young mothers-to-be are actually able to see their unborn child in the earliest weeks of development, through the hospital baby-scan. Way back in time, David had the holy insight to know that God had known him when he was made in secret, in his mother's womb. 'Fearfully and wonderfully made' is the expression he chooses.

We are told in this psalm that in the book of God every part of the human body is written, so that we may understand the preciousness of the very thoughts of God towards us. David writes, 'If I should count them, they are more in number than the sand'. This is a psalm of wonderment to those who love God and feel deep need of His constant presence. It brings tremendous consolation, and assurance and peace.

To many folk, on the contrary, whose hearts are far from God, there is a natural fear of meeting Him. His all-seeing vision is not at all welcome; more like a menace or a threat. These have not yet come into the knowledge of His peace, freely offered in the Lord Jesus. That peace is already made through the Blood shed on His Cross.

How can we make men and women of our day conscious of the great truth that they do not have to 'make their peace with God' (to use their own words) but that it is already made for them by Jesus Himself? That the dear Heavenly Father is waiting for them to come and receive this gift of love? How precious are His thoughts toward us, as sinners! 'Such knowledge is too wonderful for me'. But it is gloriously true . . . . and personal.

DAY 22

Psalm 19, v.1

The heavens declare the Glory of God.

It takes the immensity of the Heavens above to declare the Glory of God; and the firmament shows to us His handiwork. When we bunch together all that great travellers have seen on this earth, photographed and shared with others, it would only amount to a small particle of God's glory. Folk in U.S.A. would give us the best summing-up in these words, 'Boy! you ain't seen nuthin' yet!'

We look at our world today and our hearts are saying, 'why does everything change so rapidly? Where have the good standards gone?' Art, music, plays, books conceived in these last days of the twentieth century all seem to be tarnished and spoiled. Tarnished with sin in every form; obsession to the point of nausea, excessive beyond the point of no return.

Christian! We must 'look up!' Look up to the Heavens, by sunlit day and starry night. We must see the Glory of God as the psalmist did in his day. He declares, 'The heavens are telling Jehovah's Glory'.

So — they have a voice! Their voice can be heard. By whom? By you and me, by the man in the Arctic wastes, the woman in the strange culture of Tibet, and there's a man who spoke to us when he set foot on the moon! He saw, God's handiwork and he understood the words of Genesis 1. 'In the beginning God created the heaven and the earth'.

In this psalm we read that 'everybody can know'. 'There is no speech or language where their voice is not heard'. This refers to the heavens. In verse 6 there is a fresh revelation, and this is repeated in Isaiah 40, v.22. We read about 'the circuit of the earth'.

Isaiah says 'It is He that sitteth upon the circle of the earth'.

The truth, well-known today, was unknown in the day of Columbus. This man declared that the world was round and after mighty opposition, set out boldly in his ship to prove it. Columbus was a Christian and believed these verses he had evidently discovered in his Bible. He found the new land and was honoured before all the scoffers. He put faith into action!

God Himself will honour you and me too, as we consistently make discoveries in His Word, believe it, and put some action into our profession of faith.

DAY 23

Psalm 40, v.2

He brought me up also out of an horrible pit, out of the miry clay . . . .

In the first three verses of this psalm David testifies to a tremendous change in his life. He has come 'from the mire into the choir'. It all began as he waited patiently for the Lord to hear his desperate cry. Then we see the dramatic events as typified by this man in a horrible pit of noise, struggling to get a foothold on impossible substance — pictured vividly as miry clay. I wonder if you have ever come across what is known as slipper sand on shores in the south of England? If you have suddenly paddled your feet into this on a dreamy summer day, you will know the panic experience that losing your foothold brings. You struggle with your feet and clutch at the air with your hands and unless there is a friend nearby to help, you cannot get out of this treacherous place.

So here is a vivid picture in these verses of the powerful Friend of sinners, The Lord Jesus Himself, taking hold of one who has no strength to pull himself up. He is the only One who can rescue us when we are in a slippery place, because we know this is true, we cry to God and He sets our feet upon a Rock. More than this, Christ establishes the believer in a new way of life and puts a new song in his mouth; this is a song of praise and a promise goes with it.

'I'm not in the choir' you may be saying and this may be the case but note the words in verse 3 which tells us that many shall see this praising song and fear, and shall trust in the Lord. That is the promise, lay hold of it! You can see a man or woman — or even a child — who has a song in their heart, it's something so lovely that you will never forget it. Remember this psalm speaks of a new song that only God can give. He puts it in our cleansed heart and it is just Praise, Praise to His wonderful deliverance all the way!

'On Christ the solid Rock I stand,
All other ground is sinking sand'.

DAY 24

Psalm 22, v.1

My God, my God, why hast Thou forsaken me?

Forsaken! What a terrible cry! Think on this word. 'Forsaken', the depths of despair it conjures up in the mind. We find David here anointed with the spirit of prophecy and he transports us to the foot of the Cross. There we gaze upon our Saviour and we hear this anguished cry. 'My God, my God, why hast Thou forsaken me?' There was only one such moment in time when men's sins were laid upon Jesus, the Lamb of God, who carried them away for ever — the sins of the whole world. Your sin and my sin! Laid upon Him, Jesus the willing sacrifice. His Father in heaven could not even look upon Him at that moment. He is a Holy God who cannot look upon a man's sin. So the cry pierced the darkness . . . .'Forsaken!' 'Forsaken!'

This takes us to a word in Isaiah, where in chapter 54, v.6 we see the nation of Israel likened to 'a woman forsaken and grieved in spirit . . . . for a small moment have I forsaken you, but with great mercies will I gather you'. A vital truth concerning these precious chosen people of God, and a tremendous promise of restoration. This next event our world is waiting to see. God is faithful, He is the Lord, their Redeemer. 'All the ends of the world shall remember and turn unto the Lord, all the nations shall worship and bow down before Him, for the kingdom is the Lord's! So David writes down for you and me to read this vision of a not-too-distant future. 'At the name of Jesus every knee shall bow' writes Paul in his letter to the Philippian church. So we see how our Bible is all of one piece, there is no contradiction anywhere. Hallelujah! Our Jesus who suffered in our place was raised on Easter Day because He made the one great sufficient sacrifice for sin, and the Resurrection is the mighty proof that God the Father was satisfied.

Do you know what it is to feel forsaken, unforgiven, deserted by your friends and by God? We live in a day when many a wife, many husbands, know the meaning of this word 'Forsaken'. . . . far worse than losing a beloved partner through death . . . . 'Forsaken' is bitter as gall. I would point such a poor lonely one to our Jesus as He cried to His Father on that Cross. As you look, remember that He knows your sorrows and has obtained for you, personally, eternal forgiveness and a new Resurrection Life. God has not forsaken you. He is just waiting for you to turn to Him.

'There is Life for a look at the crucified One.
There is Life at this moment for you'.

DAY 25

Psalm 119, v.117

Hold thou me up and I shall be safe.

How many folk around us are not in the Kingdom, not members of any Christian fellowship and not rejoicing in any hope for their future life because of one important reason? They are afraid quite sincerely, to make any commitment to Christ because — to use their own words 'They will never be able to keep it up! And they are right! Not one of us would be able to stand firm in our faith unless God Himself held us up. Understanding our own human weakness, we have been praying this prayer with the psalmist 'Hold thou me up and I shall be safe.'

In Peter's first letter we have those words, 'We are kept by the power of God, through faith, unto salvation, ready to be revealed in the last time' *(1 Peter 1, v.5)*. What comfort to know our powerful Saviour is able to same to the uttermost, and also to KEEP that which we have committed to Him! Paul believed this and said so in 1 Timothy 1, v.12.

I wonder if you say so when folks make comments like 'I wish I had your faith' This is when we must give the right answer and tell how we know we are upheld and kept by the mighty hand of God.

The psalmist speaks, too, of God being for him a hiding place and a shield. Is not this exactly your need — and mine — from time to time? A hiding place and a shield to shelter us from the fierce storms of life. When we speak to our friends and neighbours of a God who has become all this to us, I

51

believe we shall be telling out just what they are longing to hear. Not another challenge, but a Guide, a Comforter, to whom we run in our distress, who holds us up and keeps us in safety.

We are now living in the day foretold by our Lord Jesus in Luke 21 when 'men's hearts are failing them for fear and for looking after those things that are coming on the earth'. Yes, we are into the nuclear age and hearts are really fearful, Let us be up to date, Christian, and tell of God's great loving Hand outstretched, to hold and to shield.
'Hold thou me up and I shall be safe'.

DAY 26

Psalm 73, v.25

Whom have I in heaven but Thee?

Here we have a man writing of a real problem that is as up-to-date as today's newspaper. I am at a loss to know which verse to choose in my brief comments; there is so much here that speaks of Christian experience. We will however, begin with the word in verse 1, 'God is good, to the clean of heart' and then consider the last verse, which says 'it is good for me to draw near to God'. In between these profound thoughts, simply expressed, we find a modern conflict of mind. Here is a man on the verge of backsliding. In verse 2 he tells us he has nearly lost his foothold of faith, his heart was filled with a great big question 'Why?'

'Why, God?' is the word that brings believers into this slippery place, and this may come to each one of us at times of crisis in our life. 'Why has this happened to me?' is our common reaction to sorrow; we are one with the psalmist in our dilemma. His particular point of testing came as he looked at the prosperity of the wicked around him; even corrupt and violent men seem in his eyes, to be doing well in the world. These people are proud, loaded with worldy possessions they are openly anti-God . . . . yet they seem to have everything! So he admits to being 'envious at the foolish'; those who clearly prosper in the world, they say 'How does God know?'

The thoughts of this believer form into the everlasting 'Why?' and it all becomes too painful for him. This is a depth of temptation too much for any of us to bear. BUT — he finds the answer and in verse 17 we read, 'I went into the sanctuary of God: then I understood their end.' Our psalmist finally seeks the quiet place, he makes time for his God to speak to him, to show the desolation that really awaits the unbeliever. He realises the difference in the hope and joy that the salvation of God has freely given to him; his foolishness and ignorance then grieve his heart. No wonder he cries, 'Whom have I in Heaven but Thee? and there is none upon earth that I desire beside Thee'.

Full restoration of faith is declared in the final verses 25-28. 'God is the strength of my heart and my portion for ever. . . I have put my trust in the Lord God'.

DAY 27

Psalm 81, v.10

Open thy mouth wide, and I will fill it.

This is the Lord God speaking to His people. He is reminding the children of Israel of their tremendous deliverance from the land of Egypt, how He delivered them from bondage. No wonder this psalmist begins with a shout of praise! 'Sing aloud make a joyful noise! Bring all the instruments of music — blow the trumpet!' So he admonishes God's people.

These verses lead on to the promises of God, one of which is quoted above. Sometimes as believers we do not feel like opening our mouth to sing and praise, we feel heavy and dull, yet when we join with other worshippers we find that as we do open our mouth God fills it with singing! And this does us good. Another time we may be faced with opportunity to witness for our Lord and again, the flesh is heavy and unwilling to say a word. But the promise still stands, and you and I can experience today that God is true and as we open our mouth to speak a word of testimony the message does flow and it comes from our heart.

Have you experienced times when you cannot even pray? Saying familiar words is not true prayer; we are conscious of this, but as we have the desire to pray and open our mouth wide, so God the Holy Spirit will indeed fill our hearts with the needs of people we know, and once more we shall prove this lovely promise 'Open your mouth wide and I will fill it,' with prayer.

In the book of Malachi we are challenged by

Almighty God to prove Him. In chapter 3 and verse 10 we get these words, 'Prove me now herewith, saith the Lord of Hosts if I will not open you the windows of Heaven, and pour you out a blessing that there shall not be room enough to receive it'.

You can write two letters beside this promise of blessing, 'T' and 'P' (meaning Tried and Proved) when it's become true for you. I pray you may write this many, many times. God is waiting for us to prove Him.

DAY 28

Psalm 18, v.2

The Lord is my Rock, and my fortress.

Here we have David speaking as a soldier. This psalm opens with his declaration of love for his Lord, who is his strength, his rock, his fortress, his deliverer. God is the One who buckles on David's armour. He is the high tower into which he shelters and is saved from his enemies. All this — and more — is the mighty God to David. Words cannot express all that God means to him; in another place he speaks of God as his 'hiding place', a thought that even little children can understand.

We look to the beginning of our Bible and there we have Moses in Deuteronomy 32 telling us that 'He is the Rock, His work is perfect'. He speaks of honey, oil, butter, fat and milk all being provided out of this Rock. Honey, sweetness, out of a Rock! It seems incredible, and yet we know the symbol of Moses striking that Rock and out of it flowed streams in the desert, life-giving water for thirsty men! What a picture of our Lord and Saviour, Jesus Christ, the Rock of our Salvation! He and He alone can bring the sweetness of honey, the water, oil and milk to give life and nourishment for our body, soul and spirit. In psalm 81 we hear God speaking to His people, 'With honey out of the rock should I have satisfied you'. But they had turned after other gods and would have none of Him!

Is this so amazing? We live today in a generation of men and women seeking after anything, just anything, to satisfy their lusts and desires of the flesh. No thought for their precious soul and spirit, no time for the Risen Christ, no thought for Eternity! But there's fear deep down.

All through the years, right through the scriptures, we can see Christ Himself as the solid unchanging Rock on which we may stand, a place where we may shelter from the raging storms of life. A well-loved hymn writer gave us these words:—

'Rock of ages, cleft for me,
Let me hide myself in Thee'

Turn to the New Testament and you will hear the apostle Peter as he cries, 'Thou art the Christ, Son of the Living God'. Jesus answers, 'Upon this Rock I will build my Church'. Christ Himself is the Rock on which we must build our faith, not the man Peter. The apostle Paul adds his witness to this great truth. He says in *1 Corinthians 10, v.4*, 'Our fathers drank of that spiritual Rock that followed them: and that Rock was Christ'.

DAY 29

Psalm 37, v.4

Delight thyself also in the Lord; and He shall give Thee the desires of thine heart.

I have likened these blessings from God's word to a bouquet of rich, colourful flowers. Surely this precious verse would be the perfect rose glowing in the midst! 'He shall give you the desires of your heart.' Your heart and mine are filled with strong desires, some we have waited to see fulfilled over many years. There is, perhaps, a sigh that escapes our lips as we think how long we have been waiting for these wishes to come true.

When we are born again of God's Holy spirit and Jesus is really the King of our life, a wonderful thing happens. Our deepest desires are changed! We find we have the mind of Christ taking over the old selfish, fleshly nature and giving us an overwhelming love and concern for the precious souls of those for whom He died. So these longings take precedence and the selfish motives begin to disappear. Thus God is able to give us this beautiful promise, to fulfil it and to add to this many a bonus. We who are older can testify to this, as our job is to encourage the immature, impatient younger pilgrims on the road.

Do notice the first part of this verse; do not overlook this important provision for receiving the promise. David speaks in verse 3 of this psalm of 'trusting' and then of 'committing your way.' In the midst he counsels us to 'Delight yourself also in the Lord' and this is the key that unlocks the door to the fulfilment of our longings.

We must ask ourselves some questions. (1) Do I love the quiet hour spent with God's word and in prayer for others? (2) Do I choose the company and fellowship of those who love Christ? (3) Am I most happy and blessed when I am conscious of His Presence?

This is not talk of doing good works or being busy all the time. This is a promise to be claimed by those who love God with the whole heart and really delight to be more in His company than with anything this world can offer. Then — Oh glorious prospect!—Jesus Himself will delight to give you the deep desires of your heart. And look, too, for some joys you secretly long for . . . . these come as an extra bonus.

DAY 30

Psalm 37, v.35

I have seen the wicked in great power and spreading himself like a green bay tree.

David writes:— 'I have been young, and now am old; yet I have not seen the righteous forsaken, nor his children begging bread'. He has seen much history being made in his long life; he has seen the wicked in great power, yet he passed away, disappeared from the scene, he looked for him and he could not be found!

I have a list of names of men, in recent world history noted against this scripture. My readers will recall them too. They raged, they shouted, they threatened, they created havoc in their short day, they spread themselves like a vigorous green tree . . . . but where are they today? One looks for them and, praise God, they are gone! The shouting, the raging is over and these men are facing the judgment of God. One of the most frightening verses occurs in this book of psalms; here in verse 13 and prominently in psalm 2. It states, 'The Lord shall laugh at him; for he sees that his day is coming'. In the 1st chapter of the book of Proverbs v.26 we read these words, 'I also will laugh at your calamities, I will mock when your fear comes'. Are we asking why our God of love does laugh at wicked men? He gives us the answer in this first chapter of Proverbs verse 24. It is, 'Because I have called and you refused; I have stretched out my Hand, and no man regarded'.

So will the day of fear come to these who by-passed the Living God; their destruction will come as a whirlwind, writes Solomon; indeed these unbelievers will call upon God but He tells them He will not answer. They shall then seek Him, but will not find Him. They did not choose the fear of the Lord. God tells us 'they would have none of His counsel: they despised all His reproof'.

When the Son of God came He was despised and rejected of men. They sent Him to that Cross. So men today are rejecting Christ. The Bible tells us 'They are without Christ, having no hope, and without God in the world' *(Ephesians 2, v.12)*.

DAY 31

Psalm 84, v.11

'For the Lord God is a sun and shield; the Lord will give grace and glory; no good thing will He withhold from them that walk uprightly'.

Grace and Glory! A Sun and a Shield! What perfect provision for every day of a believer's life. What more do we need? The grace of God is even given to enable you and I to walk uprightly, for this we cannot do apart from the power of the Holy Spirit inside us. In the New Testament we have Paul — that great Christian — putting this truth 'in a nutshell'. He tells us, 'The life I now live I live by the faith of the Son of God, who loved me and gave Himself for me' *(Galatians 2, v.20)*. He is speaking of his new life in Christ and the dramatic change he experienced. Paul never missed an opportunity to tell his story, even before Kings and governors.

When King David wrote of his thrilling experiences way back in time, he tells us that those who live to the praise and glory of God go 'from strength to strength'. They prove that God gives sunshine, healing, and warmth. He is the sun of righteousness who will 'arise with healing in his wings' *(Malachi 4, v.2)*. He is a shield when the winds of sorrow and adversity are blowing on our frail human lives. We must all pass through valleys — of despair, loneliness, failure and frustration; it would seem there is no escape. But David's God and the God of the Apostle Paul, and your God and mine will make the valley to be rich, fertile and productive in the believer's life.

Are you seeking for sunshine today? are you needing the protection of God's shield over your life? The Lord will give grace and glory; in fact your Heavenly Father will hold back nothing that will be good for you. How we need the grace of God for daily living! We want to live to His glory. Our desire is to walk obediently, to please Him. And one Glorious Day, when the Lord Jesus returns, we are going to pass into Glory, for ever.

'His servants shall serve Him and they shall see His face' *(Revelation 23, v.3,4)*.

> 'We shall see His lovely face,
> One bright golden morning'.